MAGIC CASTLE READERS®

Away Went the Farmer's Hat

A book about an adventure

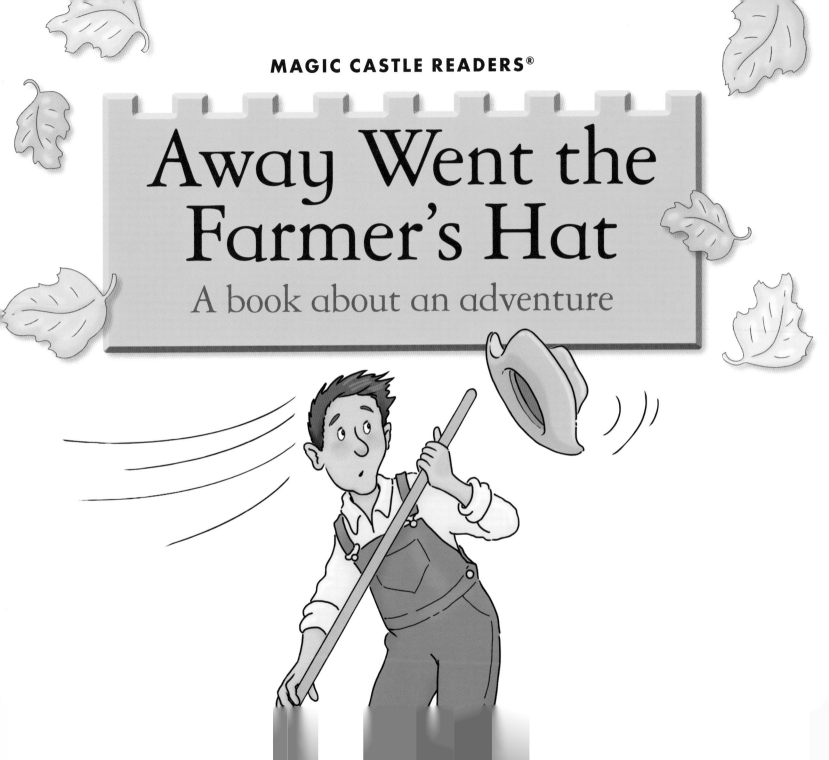

The Child's World

Published by The Child's World®
1980 Lookout Drive • Mankato, MN 56003-1705
800-599-READ • www.childsworld.com

Acknowledgments
The Child's World®: Mary Berendes, Publishing Director
The Design Lab: Design
Jody Jensen Shaffer: Editing

ISBN 9781623235727
LCCN 2013931388

Printed in the United States of America
Mankato, MN
July 2013
PA02177

Did you know...

A library is a magic castle with many Word Windows in it?

What is a Word Window?

If you said, "A book," you're right!

A book is a Word Window because the words and pictures let you look and see many things. Books are your windows to the wide, wide world around you.

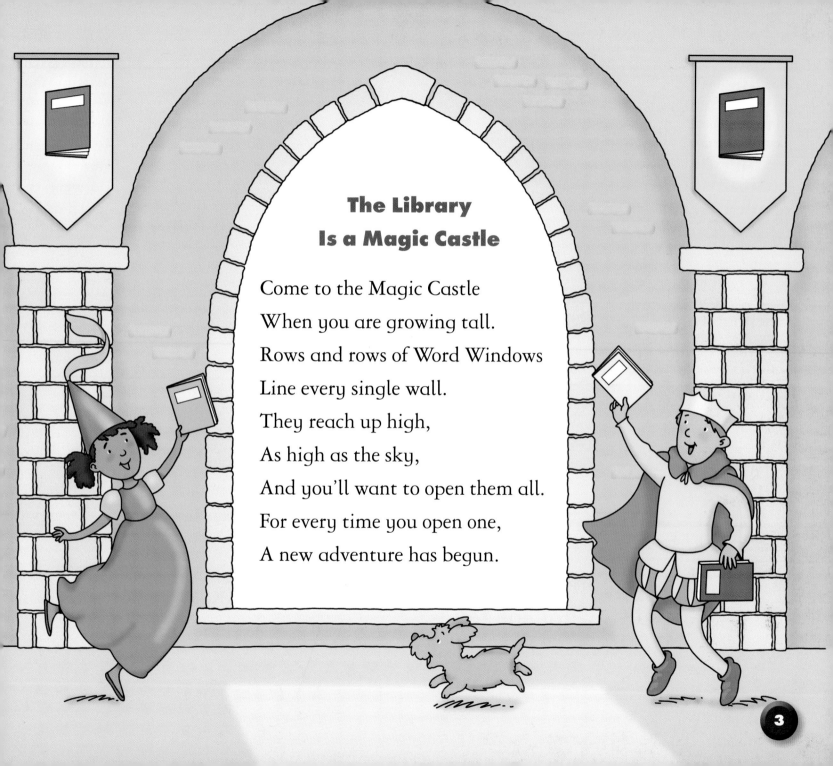

The Library
Is a Magic Castle

Come to the Magic Castle
When you are growing tall.
Rows and rows of Word Windows
Line every single wall.
They reach up high,
As high as the sky,
And you'll want to open them all.
For every time you open one,
A new adventure has begun.

Mary opens a Word Window.
Guess what she reads.

A farmer was in his field one day.
The wind blew the farmer's hat off his head.
Away went the hat.

The hat went up and around and down.
It landed on a horse's head.
"What a fine hat," the horse said.

The horse wore the hat, but not for long.
The wind blew the hat off his head, too.
Away went the hat.

The hat went up and around and down.
It landed on a pig's head.
"What a fine hat," the pig said.

The pig wore the hat, but not for long.
The wind blew the hat off her head, too.
Away went the hat.

The hat went up and around and down.
It landed on a cow's head.
"What a fine hat," the cow said.

The cow wore the hat, but not for long.
The wind blew the hat off her head, too.
Away went the hat.

The hat went up and around and down.
It landed on a goat's head.
"What a fine hat," the goat said.

The goat wore the hat, but not for long.
The wind blew the hat off her head, too.
Away went the hat.

The hat went up and around and down.
It landed in a stream.
"What a fine boat," a little duck said.

The duck floated along in the hat.

Then she came to a waterfall.
Down went the hat.

The hat went down and around
and into the high grass.

A rabbit came by. "My, what a fine nest
for my babies," said the rabbit.

The baby rabbits stayed in the farmer's hat,
but not for long.

They hopped away, one by one.
Now the hat was empty.

Then the wind blew the hat into the air.

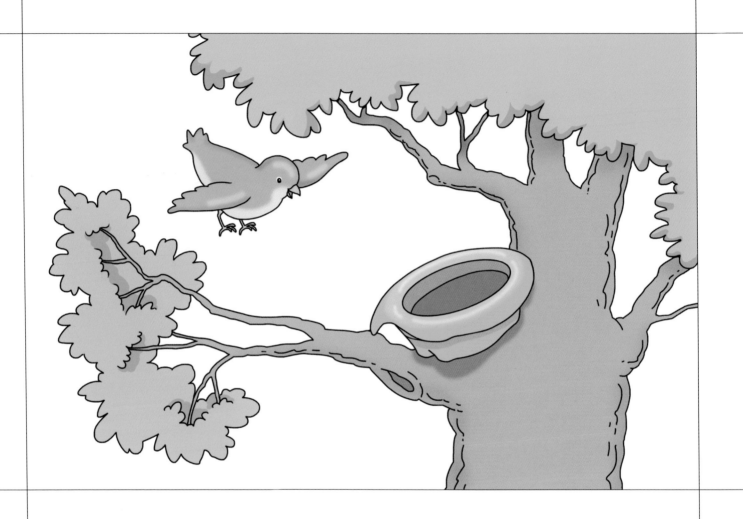

The hat went up and around and down.
It landed in a tree. A bird flew by.
"My," said the bird. "What a fine nest
for my babies."

The baby birds stayed in the farmer's hat,
but not for long. They flew away, one by one.

Then a squirrel came by. "My, what a fine nest for my babies," she said.

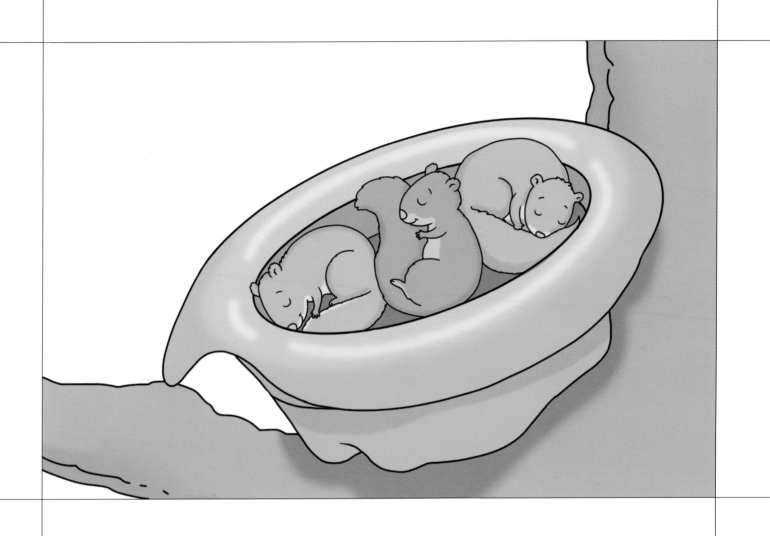

The baby squirrels stayed in the farmer's hat,
but not for long.

They climbed out of the hat, one by one.
They ran down the tree.

Now the hat was empty.
Soon the farmer came riding by.

"My hat in a tree? How can that be?"
asked the farmer.

He pulled it down. He held the hat on his head all the way home.

His wife tied two strings to his hat.

"These," she said, "will keep the hat
on your head where it belongs!"

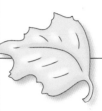

Questions and Activities

(Write your answers on a sheet of paper.)

1. Where does this story happen?
   Name two important things about that place.

2. Baby rabbits and baby birds find the farmer's hat.
   How are the baby rabbits and baby birds similar in this story?
   How are they different?

3. Did this story have any words you don't know?
   How can you find out what they mean?

4. Where did the farmer find his hat again?
   How did the hat get there?

5. Tell this story to a friend. Take only two minutes.
   Which parts did you share?